The WILDERNESS of DIVORCE

Also by Alan Wolfelt:

Healing Your Grieving Heart: 100 Practical Ideas

*Healing A Friend's Grieving Heart: 100 Practical Ideas for
Helping Someone You Love Through Loss*

The Journey Through Grief: Reflections on Healing

*Transcending Divorce: Ten Essential Touchstones for
Finding Hope and Healing Your Heart*

*The Transcending Divorce Journal:
Exploring the Ten Essential Touchstones*

*The Transcending Divorce Support Group Guide:
Meeting Plans for Facilitators*

Companion
P R E S S

Companion Press is dedicated to the education and support of both the
bereaved and bereavement caregivers. We believe that those who companion
the bereaved by walking with them as they journey in grief have a wondrous
opportunity: to help others embrace and grow through grief—and to lead
fuller, more deeply-lived lives themselves because of this important ministry.

For a complete catalog and ordering information, write or call:

Companion Press
The Center for Loss and Life Transition
3735 Broken Bow Road, Fort Collins, CO 80526
(970) 226-6050
www.centerforloss.com

The WILDERNESS of DIVORCE

Finding Your Way

Alan D. Wolfelt, Ph.D.

Companion
PRESS
Fort Collins, Colorado
An imprint of the Center for Loss and Life Transition

Companion Press is an imprint of the
Center for Loss and Life Transition,
3735 Broken Bow Road, Fort Collins, Colorado 80526
970-226-6050
www.centerforloss.com

Printed in India

17 16 15 14 13 12 11 10 09 08   5 4 3 2 1

ISBN 13: 978-1-879651-53-1

To those who have allowed me the honor of companioning them into and through the wilderness of divorce

Contents

Introduction and Welcome

Very few relationships in our human experience are more significant than the relationship we call marriage. For this reason, few life experiences are more difficult than the ending of what was once an intimate relationship.

Divorce brings a multitude of emotions and responsibilities that may seem overwhelming. A new home may need to be created. Your finances may be difficult and stressful to manage. If you have children, they will naturally have difficult questions. You may feel alone or emptied out. You may feel as if you are not only losing your marriage but also yourself. You may struggle with knowing who you are and wonder how you will survive this major life change. You may question what your future holds.

Because of the overwhelming changes that divorce brings, moving forward will take time and hard work. It will require that you are patient with yourself as you explore your old life and slowly work to create a new life. While this is naturally draining and challenging, the good news is that it is possible, and, *you are not alone*. Millions of people have experienced divorce and survived, and so will you!

The ten touchstones

In this book I describe ten Touchstones that are essential physical, emotional, cognitive, social, and spiritual actions for you to take if your hope is to integrate your divorce and find renewed meaning and purpose in your life.

Think of the grief from your divorce as a wilderness —a vast, mountainous, inhospitable forest. You are in the midst of unfamiliar and often brutal surroundings. You are cold and tired. Yet, you must journey through this wilderness. To find your way out, you must become acquainted with its terrain and learn to follow the sometimes hard-to-find trail markers that lead to healing, restoration, and eventually, transcendence.

In the wilderness of your divorce grief, the Touchstones are your trail markers. They are the signs that you are on the right path.

Open to the Presence of Your Loss

"A wound that goes unacknowledged and
unwept is a wound that cannot heal."

John Eldredge

You are going through or have experienced a divorce.

In your heart, you have come to know deep pain. From my own divorce experience as well as those of people I have companioned over the years, I have learned that we cannot go around the pain that is the wilderness of our grief surrounding lost love. Instead, we must journey all through it, sometimes shuffling along the less strenuous side paths, sometimes plowing directly into the dark center.

In many ways, and as strange as it may seem, this book is intended to help you honor the pain that comes with your divorce. You have probably been taught that pain means something is wrong and that you should find ways to alleviate the pain. In our culture, pain and feelings of loss are experiences most people try to avoid.

But you will probably learn over time that the pain of your divorce grief will keep trying to get your attention until you have the courage to gently, and in small doses, open to its presence. The alternative—denying or suppressing your pain—is in fact more painful.

Staying open to the ripple effects of divorce

During and after a divorce, there is often a huge ripple effect of additional loss that spreads out in many directions.

- *Loss of dreams and goals.* Many aspects of hopes and dreams you had together as a couple are now changed and different.
- *Loss of self-esteem.* When you experience divorce loss, it is natural that your self-esteem is impacted. You may not feel as attractive and desirable as you once did.
- *Loss of identity, belonging and lifestyle.* You were part of a "couple" and a "family." Divorce can leave you feeling uncertain of your identity and leave you questioning where you "belong" in the world around you.
- *Loss of personality.* In part, you knew who you were because you had a "mirror" in your life. When you lose your mirror, you may find yourself reflecting, "I just don't feel like myself."
- *Loss of feeling loved and accepted.* Love is anchored in acceptance. The loss of love can put you at risk for feeling unacceptable, unlovable or unworthy of love.
- *Loss of someone to express love to.* Giving love is as important as receiving love. You may feel like you have love to

give, but no one is there to receive it.

- *Loss of intimacy needs.* You may miss someone holding you, touching you, making love with you. While this is difficult for many to acknowledge, loss of emotional, physical and sexual intimacy are tremendous losses for many divorced people.
- *Loss of companionship and a partnership.* You may have been used to doing things together that you now need to do alone. It may have been little things like watching TV together, going shopping together, just being in the same room together.
- *Loss of physical security.* You may not feel as safe living alone as you did when you lived with your spouse.
- *Loss of financial security.* You may have gone from two incomes to one income, yet have increased expenses with all the changes that come with the divorce.
- *Loss of your home.* Now you may live somewhere else and it feels very different. You may have had to downsize and miss the space you used to enjoy.
- *Loss of good credit.* You may feel like you are rebuilding your financial life, and this can leave you feeling a loss of power at a time when you may already feel helpless.

- *Loss of friends and family.* Your friendships and family relationships are no doubt impacted by the divorce. You may have been close to some of your spouse's family, but those relationships have now been cut off. Sometimes family and friends are judgmental and stop all communication or, sadly, even harass you for the decisions you have made.
- *Loss of reputation.* Does anyone whisper when you pass? Does anyone spread rumors about you or your former spouse? Sometimes with divorce there are aspects of loss of reputation that may hurt deeply.
- *Loss of faith.* You may be questioning your faith or spirituality. This can result in a lost sense of meaning and purpose in your life.
- *Loss of joy and happiness.* Some of life's most precious emotions, such as joy and happiness, can be compromised by the experience of divorce.
- *Loss of health.* Divorce can compromise your immune system and result in changes in your health. Obviously, our bodies are tied into our emotions and let us know when we are stressed out.
- *Loss of your children.* You may have lost custody or have to share custody of your children. Moving children

back and forth between homes is a loss in and of itself. Not seeing your children every day or being able to put them to bed at night is a very real loss.

- *Loss of influence over your children.* If you are not with your children as much as you were before, you can experience a loss of influence over what they see, hear and do. You may experience a parental instinct to protect them but feel helpless to do so.
- *Loss of your children's loyalty.* The reality is that sometimes children take sides around who is "right" and who is "wrong" in a divorce. Sometimes children are encouraged to choose a "side," and you feel cut off from them.
- *Loss of the hope for future children.* Perhaps you had hopes to have more children in the future. The loss that comes with divorce can also bring real loss related to future children.
- *Loss of hope for a future marriage or significant relationship.* Some divorced people feel hopeless about the possibility of meeting and committing to another mate.

Setting your intention to heal and transcend

You are on a journey that is naturally frightening, painful and often lonely. No words, written or spoken, can take away the pain you feel now. I hope, however, that this book will bring comfort and encouragement as you make a commitment to embracing that very pain.

It takes a true commitment to heal your divorce grief. Yes, you are wounded, but with commitment and intention you can and will become whole again. Intention is defined as being conscious of what you want to experience. A close cousin of "affirmation," it is using the power of positive thought to produce a desired result.

When you set your intention to heal and eventually transcend this life-changing experience, you make a true commitment to positively influence the course of your journey. Healing and integrating this loss into your life demands that you engage actively in the grief journey. It can't be fixed or resolved; it can only be soothed and integrated through actively experiencing the multitude of thoughts and feelings involved.

Integrating your divorce grief

The concept of intention-setting presupposes that your outer reality is a direct reflection of your inner thoughts and beliefs. If you can change or mold some of your thoughts and beliefs, then you can influence your reality. In journaling and speaking (and praying!) your intentions, you actively help "set" them.

You might tell yourself, "I can and will reach out for support during this difficult time in my life. I will become filled with hope that I can and will survive this divorce." Together with these words, you might form mental pictures of hugging and talking to your friends and seeing happier times in your future.

Setting your intention to heal is not only a way of surviving your divorce, it is a way of actively guiding your grief. Of course, you will still have to honor and embrace your pain during this time. By honoring the presence of your pain, by understanding the appropriateness of your pain, you are committing to facing the pain.

In reality, denying your grief, running from it, or minimizing it only seems to make it more confusing and overwhelming. Paradoxically, to eventually soften your hurt, you must embrace it. As strange as it may seem, you must make it your friend.

In this book, I will attempt to teach you to gently and lovingly befriend your divorce grief. To not be so afraid to express your grief. To not be ashamed of your tears and profound feelings of sadness. To try not to pull down the blinds that shut out light and love. Slowly, and in "doses," you can and will return to life and begin to live in ways that put stars back into your sky.

I invite you to gently confront the pain of your grief. I will try with all of my heart to point to the Touchstones as you journey through the wilderness of your divorce grief. As we go forward, remember: As you do your grief work you will experience transcendence and live with meaning and purpose every day of your life.

Dispel the Misconceptions About Divorce and Grief

"Life is like an onion. You peel it off one layer at a time, and sometimes you weep."

Carl Sandburg

As you journey through the wilderness of your divorce grief, you will come to find a path that feels right for you. This path will be your path to healing and eventual transcendence. But beware—others may try to pull you off this path. They may try to make you believe that the path you have chosen is wrong, even "crazy," and that their way is better.

The reason that people try to pull you off the path to healing is that they have internalized some common misconceptions about the divorce experience. Many of the misconceptions deny you your right to hurt and authentically mourn your lost hopes and dreams for your marriage.

Misconception: Grief and mourning are the same thing.

Perhaps you have noticed that people tend to use the words "grieving" and "mourning" interchangeably. There is an important distinction, however. We as humans move toward integrating loss (divorce loss included) into our lives not just by grieving, but by mourning.

Grief is the constellation of internal thoughts and feelings we have when we experience divorce.

Mourning is when you take the grief you have inside and express it outside of yourself. Another way of defining mourning is "grief gone public" or the "outward expression of grief."

Obviously, this book is rooted in the importance of openly and honestly mourning the loss of your relationship by expressing your grief outside of yourself. Over time and with the support of others, mourning will create momentum for your healing.

Misconception: If you get a divorce, you are a failure.

There are those people out there who may project to you that when your marriage ends, you are a failure as a person. Nothing could be further from the truth.

Divorce is about the disintegration of hopes and dreams, about a life partner who did not materialize. Divorce is not failure, it is a transition. We are conditioned by society to bring to marriage many unrealistic expectations, such as "two shall become one," "until death do us part," and, of course, "happily every after."

Actually, in a healthy partnership, two people remain separate individuals who communicate respect for each other, perceive each other as equals, and grow both individually and together. The reality is that for many, it takes more than one try to both discover and experience this kind of equal and mutually satisfying relationship.

Misconception: When you marry, you must stay committed to the thought that this love will last forever.

Many people grow up believing that one ideal person completes them and that after they find one another, they will live happily ever after.

Yet, in reality, relationships do end. No, we don't always understand why they end, but they do. About one of every two marriages ends in divorce. This fact demonstrates that love is often not forever. This misconception related to "forever" often results in us judging ourselves harshly when our relationships end.

Relationships sometimes have a lifetime of their own that does not include forever. A relationship is not always the final resting place where you settle in forever.

Misconception: If you get a divorce, you will never marry again.

Some people would have you believe that if you get a divorce, you will never have another significant relationship or marry again. However, divorce is often a transition to single-hood, re-coupling, or eventual remarriage.

The reality is that many divorced people do eventually remarry. Actually, about three out of four North Americans who get divorced remarry, usually within three years.

I have companioned many people through the divorce process: people who didn't want the relationship to end; people who initiated the end of the relationship; and people who mutually agreed to end the relationship. My experience has been that regardless of the circumstances, if you are willing to authentically mourn your loss, you can go on to create new and satisfying intimate partnerships.

Misconception: After your divorce, the goal should be to "get over it" and "move on" as quickly as possible.

Our culture tends to be impatient with experiences that involve grief, loss and the need to mourn. Don't be shocked when some people around you expect you to be "back to normal" very soon after your divorce.

If you openly express grief outwardly, you may be viewed by some as "weak," "crazy" or "self-pitying." The sometimes subtle but direct message is "shape up and get on with your life."

If you internalize these kinds of messages, you may be tempted to repress (bottle up) your thoughts and feelings about the divorce.

Remember—society will often encourage you to prematurely move away from and "get over" your divorce loss. You must continually remind yourself that leaning toward, not away from, the pain that accompanies this major life transition will actually make your eventual healing easier.

Misconception: When the grief and mourning of your divorce are integrated into your life, the painful thoughts and feelings will never come up again.

Oh if only this were so. Divorce is a process, not an event. As your experiences have probably already taught you, grief comes in and out like waves from the ocean. Sometimes when you least expect it, a huge wave comes along and pulls your feet right out from under you.

You may have your divorce decree, but that does not mean these waves stop rolling in. Sometimes heightened periods of sadness may leave you feeling overwhelmed. These times seem to come from nowhere and can be frightening and painful.

You will always, for the rest of your life, feel some aspects of grief and loss over the ending of your relationship. However, these feelings will one day no longer dominate your daily life or be the center of your life. Yet, they will always be there, in the background, reminding you of the person and the relationship you were once connected to.

Usually, the capacity to be supportive without judging is most developed in people who have been on some kind of grief journey themselves and are willing to be empathetically present to you during this difficult time.

If you find yourself around people who believe in the misconceptions outlined in this chapter, you may feel very alone. If the people you are closest to are unable to support you without judging you, seek out others who can offer nonjudgmental love and support.

Embrace the Uniqueness of Your Divorce Experience

"Whether a marriage fractures with one quick snap or dies a slow death, a powerful bond is broken."

David B. Hawkins

The wilderness of your divorce experience is *your* wilderness. It is a creation of your unique self, the unique person you were married to, and the unique circumstances of your divorce.

Despite what you may hear about what the divorce experience is like for someone else, you will encounter it in your own unique way. Consider taking a "one-day-at-a-time" approach.

This Touchstone invites you to explore some of the unique aspects of your divorce experience—the "influences" on your journey through this wilderness.

The circumstances of the divorce

There are many circumstances that can make each divorce unique. Some couples come to divorce after years of alienation, constant fighting and neglect. Or you may have felt you still loved your spouse, yet he or she suddenly announced he or she wanted a divorce. Or, perhaps you lived with your spouse for a long time after learning you were no longer loved by him or her. Maybe you realized early on in your marriage that one day it would end; you just didn't know when.

Regardless of your unique circumstances, the ending of a relationship is a naturally difficult rite of passage to a life that will be very different than before. Whether your marriage died a slow death or experienced an unexpected crisis that created an end, whether you were the "leaver" or the "left," you are now faced with a need to mourn what once was.

Your unique personality

What words would you use to describe yourself? What words would people use to describe you? Whatever your unique personality, rest assured that it will be reflected in your response to the divorce experience and the way you mourn this major life change.

If you tend to run away from stressful aspects of life, you may have an instinct to do the same thing now. If, however, you have always confronted crisis head on and openly, you may walk right into the center of the wilderness.

Other aspects of your personality, such as your self-esteem, values, and beliefs, also impact your response to divorce. In addition, any long-term problems with depression or anxiety will probably influence your grief.

The people in your life

How are the people around you supporting you at this difficult time? Mourning lost relationship dreams requires mourning, and mourning requires the outside support of others.

Without a stabilizing support system of at least one other person, the odds are that you will have difficulty doing your work of mourning. Healing requires an environment of empathy, caring, acceptance and gentle encouragement.

Your children

Whether you have young children, teenage children or adult children, you are probably concerned about how your divorce is affecting them and your relationship with them. We would be deceiving ourselves not to recognize that parental divorce is naturally difficult for children.

It is so very important to remember that even the most caring parents don't completely have it together when divorce becomes a part of their life journey. Keep in mind that all change usually starts with chaos. It is naturally difficult to be totally available and supportive to your children's emotional and spiritual needs at this time. Please don't be too hard on yourself if you make some missteps while you are in this wilderness experience. Your sincerity, consideration and love will make up for some of the difficult patches you encounter.

Your cultural/ethnic background

Your cultural and ethnic background can be an important influence on how you experience and express the grief related to your divorce. When I say culture, I mean the values, rules (spoken and unspoken), and traditions that guide you and your family. Education and political beliefs are also aspects of your cultural background (religion, too, but we'll get to that next). Often these values, rules, traditions and beliefs have been handed down generation to generation.

Your religious or spiritual background

Your personal belief system can have a tremendous impact on your divorce experience. You may discover that your religious or spiritual life is initiated, changed, deepened or renewed in some way as a result of your divorce journey. Or you may well find yourself questioning your beliefs as part of your work as you mourn your marriage.

When experiencing divorce, some people may feel very close to God or a Higher Power, while others may feel more distant and angry. Mistakenly, some people think that being "strong in faith" means you can bypass the need to mourn your divorce. Having faith does not mean you do not need to mourn your lost relationship, hopes and dreams. Having faith means having the courage to mourn your lost relationship, hopes and dreams.

Other changes, crises or stresses in your life right now

What else is going on in your life right now? While some people tend to think of divorce as a single event, it is actually a process that involves a multitude of changes and stresses. To mention a few, there are often changes in your normal routine, finances, social life, personal identity, family identity, and dreams and goals.

Whatever your specific situation, I'm sure that your divorce grief is not the only stress in your life right now. And the more intense and numerous the stresses in your life, the more overwhelmed you may feel at times.

Your physical health

How you feel physically will have a significant impact on how you cope with the stresses and changes you are experiencing. Obviously, stress and transition cause physiological changes to your body. Be aware that you may be more vulnerable to viruses and other illnesses right now.

Lack of care of your body will add more stress to your life. If you are tired and eating poorly, your coping skills will be diminished. If you are self-treating stress with alcohol or drugs, you are adding even more stress on your body. If you have a preexisting medical condition, you may notice that it is impacted or complicated by the current stress you are experiencing.

Your financial health

How is your financial health? Not only are you physically and emotionally vulnerable during this time in your life, you are economically vulnerable. You may be in intensive care related to your economic health. Some who get divorced have plenty of resources, while others have literally no means to support themselves.

Even if you feel fortunate in this area, you might be wise to get a financial check-up to help you understand your situation and plan accordingly. Fortunately, there are many resources available that can help you cope with your financial present and future.

Other factors influencing your divorce experience

What else is shaping your unique divorce experience? There are probably other factors, large and small, that are influencing your journey right now.

This Touchstone has encouraged you to explore some of the unique aspects of your divorce experience—the "influences" on your journey through the wilderness. Again, the purpose of doing this is to help you mourn what you have lost in an effort to eventually help you go forward to a life filled with meaning and purpose. I am honored to companion you on this journey.

Next, I will lead you into an exploration of some of the feelings you may be encountering during this time in your life. I have discovered that an important part of integrating divorce into your life involves listening to and attending to your inner voice, then giving expression to those thoughts and feelings as you experience them. While it may sound simplistic, I have come to know that we all have to "feel it to heal it."

Explore Your Feelings of Loss

"Only when we are no longer afraid do we begin to live."

Dorothy Thompson

Stepping into the wilderness of your many feelings is an important and sacred part of your life right now. It is my experience that we cannot heal what we cannot or do not allow ourselves to feel. Taking ownership of your wilderness emotions is the only way to eventually re-orient and transcend this major life transition.

Shock, numbness, denial, and disbelief

The first reaction for many people facing divorce loss is shock and disbelief. "It feels like a dream," people in early divorce grief often say. "I feel like I might wake up and none of this will have happened."

Thank goodness for shock, numbness and disbelief! These are not only common initial responses, but also helpful ones if they do not continue for too long. These anesthetized conditions are nature's way of temporarily protecting you from the full reality of what confronts you.

Temporarily, denial, like shock and numbness, is a great gift. It helps you survive. While denial is helpful—even necessary—early on, ongoing denial clearly blocks the path to healing. If you cannot eventually acknowledge that your marriage is over, you cannot mourn the loss and move forward with your life.

Disorganization and confusion

The divorce journey often results in experiences of restlessness, agitation, impatience, and ongoing confusion and disorganization. It's like being in the middle of a wild, rushing river where you can't get a grasp on anything.

You may express disorganization and confusion in your inability to complete tasks. You may start to do something but never finish. You may feel forgetful and ineffective, especially early in the morning and late at night, when fatigue and lethargy are most prominent. Disconnected thoughts may race through your mind and a multitude of strong emotions may be overwhelming.

When you feel disoriented, talk to someone who will be supportive and understanding. Sometimes when you talk, you may not think you make much sense. And you may not. But talking it out can still be self-clarifying, even at a subconscious level.

Anxiety, panic and fear

Feelings of anxiety, panic and fear also may be a part of your experience. Anxiety is often inevitable during times of major disruption, where what has been familiar is being replaced with an uncertain future, emotions are overwhelming, decisions are pressing, and new day-to-day problems require action.

You may ask yourself, "Am I going to be OK?" " Will I survive this?" "Will my future have some meaning and purpose?" "Will I be alone the rest of my life?" These questions are natural. Your sense of security has been threatened, so you are naturally anxious and fearful.

The good news is that expressing your feelings of anxiety, panic, and fear can help make them feel more tolerable. And knowing that they are temporary may help you during this trying time.

Explosive emotions

Anger, hate, blame, terror, resentment, rage, and even jealousy are explosive emotions that may be part of your experience. For some, unfamiliar feelings of vindictiveness and bitterness may feel like they are taking you over.

I have found that it helps to understand that all of these explosive feelings are, fundamentally, a form of *protest*. It is instinctive in the face of loss and massive change to protest—to dislike your new reality and want to change it in some way.

If explosive emotions are part of your journey (and they aren't for everyone), be aware that you have two avenues for expression—outward or inward. The outward avenue leads to eventual healing and transformation; the inward does not. Keeping your explosive emotions inside often leads to low self-esteem, depression, anxiety disorders, guilt, physical complaints and sometimes even persistent thoughts of self-destruction.

Remember—you can't go around your divorce grief, or over it, or under it—you must go through it. I hope that as you journey through grief you will be surrounded by people who understand, support and love you and will help you explore your explosive emotions without judging you or trying to stifle you.

Guilt, regret, self-blame, shame, rejection, worthlessness and failure

When the initial shock of what you are going through wears off, you may find yourself with some of the following questions: "What could I have done differently?" "Where did we go wrong?" "Am I a total failure or what?"

Similarly, some divorced people experience a serious case of the "if onlys": "If only I had been more attentive to her and pursued my career less." "If only we had spent more quality time together." "If only we hadn't had the kids so soon, so we could have gotten to know each other better."

When a relationship you once had warm, loving feelings about comes to an end, it is natural to think about actions you could have taken to change the outcome.

Learning to honor the mystery surrounding both the beginning and ending of your relationship is naturally difficult, yet necessary. The reality is that there are some things in life we cannot change. Yet, there is nothing wrong with asking yourself where things went wrong. Your soul will actually benefit from an exploration of what could have been different.

Sadness, depression, loneliness and vulnerability

Some of the most familiar aspects of divorce grief are sadness, depression, loneliness and vulnerability. Someone who was once a central part of your life is now gone. Allowing yourself to feel your sadness is in large part what your journey toward healing is all about.

You may find that certain times and circumstances make you more sad than others. These "triggers" are experiences or events that reawaken past experiences. Maybe you are driving along and "your song" comes on the radio. Maybe you see the same model of car he or she drives. Whatever your unique triggers, they often bring waves of sadness.

You also have a right to feel lonely. One person I supported noted, "Suddenly I had no one to share my meals with, my bed with, and special moments in the lives of my kids, like birthdays and holidays. I was used to having him around, and now he isn't here anymore. There is a strange emptiness in this house."

Consider that alone time also has some healing qualities. Spending time alone allows for reflection, introspection and development of your inner self. Over time and with work, your feelings of loneliness and emptiness can and will be replaced by inner fullness and gentle strength. You will have experienced some true personal growth when you are comfortable by yourself, no longer dependent on being around other people all the time.

Paradoxically, the only way to lessen your pain is to move toward it, not away from it. Find accepting and understanding people with whom you can express your authentic feelings.

Relief, release, happiness, euphoria and hope

Sometimes you may feel aspects of relief and release when you get a divorce. Some people even use the words happiness and euphoria to describe their experiences. If your relationship was full of conflict, you had irreconcilable differences, or something dramatic happened to push you apart, you may well be one of those people who feel relief when the marriage is over.

Even if you feel some initial relief when your divorce is final, you may experience rollercoaster emotions in the weeks and months ahead. Some people are sailing along and then get shocked when waves of sadness set in down the line. If this happens to you, remember there is nothing wrong with you. Instead you are discovering that mourning the loss of a relationship is experienced in a wave-like fashion.

A final thought about the feelings you may experience

As you journey through the wilderness of your grief, over time and with the support of others you will come to experience what I like to describe as "integration." When you come out on the other side of the wilderness and you are able to fully enjoy life and living again, you have encountered the integration of your divorce transition. You will learn more about this important concept in Touchstone Nine. But before we get there, let's explore some of the other trail markers to watch out for on your path to healing.

Recognize You Are Not Crazy

"When two people decide to get a divorce, it isn't a sign that they 'don't understand' one another, but a sign that they have, at last, begun to."

Helen Rowland

The two most common questions I get as a counselor to people experiencing divorce are "Am I crazy?" and "Am I normal?" Rest assured you're not going crazy, you're simply experiencing a major life transition.

Following are a number of common thoughts and feelings that may cause you to feel like you're going crazy. They may or may not be part of your personal experience.

Sudden changes in mood

The divorce journey can make you feel like you are surviving fairly well one minute and in the depths of despair the next. You are on an "emotional rollercoaster." If you have these ups and downs, don't be hard on yourself. Instead, be patient with yourself. As you allow yourself to mourn your lost relationship and move toward healing, the periods of hopelessness will be replaced by periods of hopefulness.

Lingering attachment

Many divorced people experience lingering attachment to their former spouses. It is not always so easy, even when there is good reason for a relationship to end, to simply make a clean break.

For some people, feelings of lingering attachment prevent them from getting on with life and developing a new self-identity. There are times when close proximity or shared custody of children make this experience even more naturally complicated.

If you feel a lingering attachment, it may be difficult for a while, but these feelings will ease as you do the work of mourning your lost relationship.

Rethinking and retelling the story

Often when a relationship ends, you need to think and talk about your marriage and the circumstances of the divorce. You may feel like you can't "shake" your memories of certain moments. You may replay these memories over and over in your mind and question your sanity.

You may also feel the need—almost a compulsion—to tell other people about these prominent memories again and again.

I call this natural process "storying." Telling the story isn't a sign that you are crazy; in fact, it's a sign that you're doing your work of mourning this major life change. Whether you're conscious of this fact or not, you tell yourself the story in an effort to integrate it into your life.

Self-focus

Especially early in your divorce experience, you may find yourself being less conscious of the needs of others. You may not want to listen to other people's problems. You may not have the energy for all the needs of your children or family.

If you are less tuned in to the needs of others and are instead focusing on your own thoughts and feelings, this doesn't mean you're crazy or selfish. What is does mean is that you have emotional needs demanding your attention right now. Don't feel guilty or shame yourself for these feelings. They are a necessary part of your grief work.

Powerlessness and helplessness

Your encounter with divorce can sometimes leave you feeling powerless. You may think or say, "What am I going to do? I feel so completely helpless."

You may wonder what could have been if only things were different. Could the divorce have been prevented? Could you have tried harder to make it work? These "if onlys" and "what ifs" are often expressions of wishing you could have had more control over something you could not.

By acknowledging and allowing for temporary feelings of helplessness, you actually help yourself. When you try to "stay strong," you often get yourself into trouble.

Griefbursts

A "griefburst" is a sudden, sharp feeling of grief that can result in anxiety, sadness, and pain. Some people call them grief attacks, because they seem to attack you without warning.

You might think that long periods of deep sadness characterize the typical divorce journey. Actually, more typically people encounter acute and episodic "pangs" or "spasms" of grief among less painful blocks of time.

Griefbursts may feel like "crazy bursts," but they are a normal and necessary part of the divorce experience. When and if one strikes you, be compassionate with yourself. You have every right to feel temporary paralysis or loss of control.

Crying and sobbing

Sobbing is an expression of the deep, strong emotions within you. These emotions need to get out, and sobbing allows for their release.

If you're crying or sobbing a lot, you're not crazy. Cry, wail, and sob as long and as hard and as often as you need to. Don't try to be strong and brave for yourself or anyone else. Tears have a voice of their own. You will be wise to allow yours to speak to you.

Painful linking objects and memorabilia

Linking objects and memorabilia are items that remind you of your lost relationship, such as photos, wedding rings, gifts, and clothing. These objects can naturally trigger all sorts of feelings, from sadness to resentment to intense anger. When this happens, you may feel a little out of control. Again, remember, you are not crazy, you are human, and you are allowing yourself to feel.

Consider boxing up these items up and storing them away for a while. Don't impulsively throw them all away. As time passes and you do your work of mourning, it can be helpful to go through these linking objects. Eventually, you will probably discover that they have less control over you and that you can make better decisions about what to do with them.

Dreams and nightmares

Sometimes, the process of disengaging from your spouse physically is far easier than getting him or her out of your head. Dreaming a lot about your former spouse may contribute to your feelings of going crazy.

Keep in mind that dreams are one of the ways some people do aspects of the work of mourning. You may dream of being back together and then separating again. You may replay the end of the relationship in your dreams. You may dream of being intimate with this person again.

If dreams are part of your experience, make use of them to better understand where you have been, where you are, and where you are going. Also, find a skilled listener who won't interpret your dreams to you, but who will help you discover what your dreams mean to you.

Anniversary and holiday occasions

Naturally, anniversary and holiday occasions can bring back memories of precious times, some happy, some sad. Birthdays (your ex's and your own), your wedding date, and family-oriented holidays like Easter, Thanksgiving, Hanukkah, and Christmas invite you to reflect and think of what you did together on these occasions.

If you're having a really tough time on special days, you're not crazy. Don't suffer in silence. Recognize you need support and map out how to get it.

You're not crazy, you're transitioning

Never forget that your journey through the wilderness of divorce may bring you through all kinds of strange and unfamiliar terrain. When it seems like you are going crazy, remind yourself to look for this trail marker that assures you that you're not going crazy. You are experiencing a major life transition that requires that you confront many new changes and challenges. Don't judge yourself; instead be self-loving and patient, and seek compassionate support from people around you. And remember, you will eventually get where you need to go.

Understand the Six Needs of Divorce Transition

"The capacity for hope is the most significant fact of life. It provides human beings with a sense of destination and the energy to get started."

Norman Cousins

If you are hoping for a map for your journey through the experience of divorce, none exists. *Your* wilderness is an undiscovered wilderness and you are its first explorer.

But those of us who have experienced divorce have found that our paths have many similarities. In fact, there are more commonalities than there are differences. When we experience divorce transition, we do have similar needs. Instead of referring to stages, I say that we have six central needs of divorce transition. You will probably jump around in random fashion while working on them. You will address each need when you are ready to do so. Sometimes you will be working on more than one need at a time.

Need 1: Acknowledge the reality of the divorce

You can know something in your head but not in your heart. Your emotional divorce is not the same as your legal divorce, and these often do not unfold at the same time or pace.

Whether the divorce was sudden and traumatic, or gradual and anticipated, acknowledging the full reality of the divorce may occur over weeks and months. Embracing your new reality is usually not quick, easy or efficient. Yet, it must be done so you can eventually move forward with your new life, free of the ties that bind you.

One moment the reality of the divorce may be unbearable; another moment it may be welcomed. At yet another moment, it may feel tolerable. Be patient with this need while at the same time creating some momentum to keep "dosing" yourself with your new reality.

Need 2: Let yourself feel the pain of the divorce

This need of mourning requires us to embrace the pain of our divorce experience—something we naturally don't want to do. It is easier to avoid, repress or deny the pain that accompanies this major life transition, yet it is in confronting our pain that we learn to reconcile ourselves to it.

You will probably discover that you need to dose yourself in embracing your painful symptoms that come with the journey. In other words, you cannot (nor should you try to) overload yourself with hurt all the time. Sometimes you may need to distract yourself or take a "time-out" from the pain of the divorce, while at other times you will need to create a safe place to move toward it.

As you encounter your pain, you will also need to continue to nurture yourself physically, emotionally, cognitively, socially, and spiritually. Eat well, rest often, and exercise regularly. Find others with whom you can share your painful thoughts and feelings; friends who listen without judging are your most important helpers as you work on this important need.

Need 3: Shift your relationship with your former spouse

This need of divorce transition involves disengaging from your prior relationship with your former life partner. As hard as it might be, you will have to stop interacting in old ways and work to create mutually acceptable new ways of communicating. While all of the following actions may or may not help you in your unique situation, some can probably be of help in redefining your relationship:

- Establish clear boundaries. For example, limit your contact with each other to required issues only, such as children.
- If you must communicate, formalize how you will communicate; set pre-arranged, time-limited meetings or phone calls.
- Do not involve each other in any of the functions (with the exception of parenting) that your ex had responsibility for in the marriage (laundry, bill paying, car maintenance).
- If you have children, formalize new parenting responsibilities. Arrange a schedule that details when the children will be with each of you.
- Respect the privacy of your former spouse. Do not offer up personal information and do not ask any of him or her. Remember: You are creating new boundaries.
- If you have children, learn to co-parent effectively.
- Openly acknowledge your divorce. Telling people helps you shift the relationship and remind yourself that you have started a new and changed life.
- If distorted anger directed at your former spouse has put you on hold, consider taking back control of your life through forgiveness.

Need 4: Develop a new self-identity

When you go through a divorce, your self-identity, or the way you see yourself, changes.

As a married person, you defined yourself as a couple. Divorce means you are no longer on the same team. You have gone from being a wife or a husband to a single woman or a single man who has lost a large part of your identity. The way you define yourself and the way society defines you is changed.

Many people find that as they work on this need, they ultimately discover some positive aspects of their changed identity. When your relationship has ended, you may realize how much of yourself you may have disowned, given away or invested in your spouse or in the relationship itself. Think of it this way: Divorce reintroduces you to yourself.

Need 5: Search for meaning

When you experience a divorce, you naturally question the meaning and purpose of life. You will probably take a good, hard look at where you see yourself now and in the future. You may question your philosophy of life and explore religious and spiritual values as you work on this need. You will instinctively revisit your account of your marriage and divorce. "What went wrong?" "Why us?" "What could we have done differently?"

If you do your grief work, you will see movement through this search for meaning and discover new life. But I have found it cannot be hurried. Your new life vision must come in its own time and you must allow it to unfold.

As you search for meaning and purpose, you are ready to make short- and long-term goals. What is important to you? Do you eventually want another love relationship? What are your financial needs and how do you accomplish them? Are you becoming the person you want to be? Creating new life goals is part of your search for meaning and purpose.

Need 6: Let others help you—now and always

The quality and quantity of understanding support you get during your divorce experience will have a major influence on your capacity to integrate this major transition into your life. You cannot—nor should you try to—go through this alone and in isolation.

Unfortunately, because our society places so much value on "putting the past in the past," "moving forward" and "letting go," divorced men and women don't always receive ongoing support. People who see your experience as something that should be quickly overcome instead of experienced will not help you integrate your divorce into your life.

To be truly helpful, the people in your support system must recognize and appreciate the impact the divorce has had on you. They must understand that in order to eventually go forward in life, you must be allowed—even encouraged—to mourn your lost relationship.

The beauty of right now

As you actively work on these six needs, you will become open to the beauty that surrounds you right now. You can be self-compassionate and experience the capacity for joy in your life. Now you can have gratitude that you entered into the wilderness of your divorce experience. Now you can be grateful that you've discovered the meaning of life and living fully in the moment, while not being bound by your past. What a gift!

Nurture Yourself

"Like a broken bone, the emotional wounds
of divorce need to be x-rayed, reset, and
given time to heal properly. The patient
has to learn a new routine and is given
permission to stay off her feet for a while."

Florence Littauer

I remind you that when you experience divorce, you have some special needs. Perhaps one of the most important special needs right now is to be compassionate with yourself—to honor this season of tenderness in your life. In fact, the word "compassion" means "with passion." Caring for and about yourself with passion is self-compassion.

Over many years of walking with people in the wilderness of divorce, I have discovered that most of us are hard on ourselves during this time in our lives. We judge ourselves. We shame ourselves. And we often take care of ourselves last. But good self-care is essential to your survival.

Nurturing yourself in five important realms

When we have special needs, one of our most important needs is to nurture ourselves in five important areas:

- physically
- emotionally
- cognitively
- socially
- spiritually

What follows is a brief introduction to each of these areas.

The physical realm

Divorce ranks among the most stressful life events you can experience. This means you have an increased risk of illness, exhaustion, and depleting your body's resources during this time in your life.

Among the most common physical responses to the stress that accompanies divorce are troubles with sleeping and low energy. During this journey you are on, your body needs more rest than usual.

Muscle aches and pains, shortness of breath, feelings of emptiness in your stomach, tightness in your throat or chest, digestive problems, sensitivity to noise, heart palpitations, queasiness, nausea, headaches, increased allergies, changes in appetite, weight loss or gain, agitation, and generalized tension—these are all ways your body may react to your divorce.

Excellent self-care is important at this time. The quality of your life ahead depends on how you take care of your body today. Divorce brings an awareness of the reality that you are individually responsible for all aspects of your life, especially your health and well-being.

The emotional realm

We explored in Touchstone Four a multitude of emotions that are often part of the divorce journey. These emotions reflect that you often have special needs that require support from both outside yourself and inside yourself. Becoming familiar with the terrain of these emotions can and will help you integrate the divorce transition into your life. The important thing to remember is that we honor our emotions when we give attention to them.

The cognitive realm

Your mind has the intellectual ability to think, absorb information, make decisions and reason logically. Just as your body and emotions let you know you have special needs, your mind does too.

Being able to consistently think normally when impacted by divorce would be very unlikely. Don't be surprised if you struggle with short-term memory problems, have trouble making even simple decisions and think you may be going crazy. Essentially, your mind is in a state of disorientation and confusion.

Your mind needs time to catch up with what you are experiencing. Be gentle with yourself right now and don't expect too much of yourself in this cognitive area of functioning.

The social realm

Naturally, divorce can sometimes leave you feeling disconnected from the outside world. Having a support system of friends and family you can count on is vital. When you reach out and connect with friends and family, you are beginning to reconnect.

If you don't nurture the warm, loving relationships that still exist in your life, you run the risk of feeling disconnected and isolated. Some people withdraw into their own small world and end up grieving the divorce, but not mourning. I don't want that to be you!

The spiritual realm

I realize that the word spiritual has many different meanings to different people. For our purposes here, I think of spirituality as the collection of beliefs that make sense of our existence.

Your spiritual encounter with divorce often invites new questions about your past, your present, and your future. You naturally go on a search to understand your lost relationship and may discover a perspective that places life in the context of something bigger than your day-to-day existence.

Nurturing a spiritual life invites you to connect with nature and the people around you. Your heart opens and your life takes on renewed meaning and purpose. You are filled with compassion for other people, particularly those who have walked the path of divorce. You become kinder, more gentle, and more forgiving of others as well as yourself.

Practicing self-compassion

We've explored five realms of self-care during this naturally difficult time in your life: physical, emotional, cognitive, social, and spiritual. If you care for yourself "with passion" in all five realms, you will find your journey through the wilderness of divorce much more tolerable. So be good to yourself.

Finding others who will be good to you is also critically important. You can't walk this path alone. In the next chapter, I'll help you reach out for help.

Reach Out for Help

"I get by with a little help from my friends."

John Lennon

During this challenging time of major transition in your life, nothing can take the place of a caring community of supportive others.

Carefully selected friends and family members can often form the core of your support system. Reach out to others. Do not make the mistake of totally withdrawing because you don't want to "burden" people. Look for family and friends who can provide you non-judgmental support.

Be careful not to express what you are going through to anyone and everyone all the time, however. If you find yourself talking with anyone and everyone about your divorce and seeking their support, I encourage you to see a professional counselor who can help you sort out what you are experiencing. If you don't seek additional help, some of your family and friends may begin to avoid you, and the result will be that you feel rejected or abandoned.

Dr. Wolfelt's rule of thirds

In my own divorce experience and in the lives of people I have been privileged to counsel, I have discovered that in general, you can take all the people in your life and divide them into thirds when it comes to emotional support.

One third of the people in your life will turn out to be neutral in response to your divorce experience. They will neither help nor hinder you in your journey.

Another third of the people in your life will turn out to be harmful to you in your efforts to integrate the divorce into your life. While they are usually not setting out to intentionally harm you, they will judge you, give you unsolicited advice, minimize your experience, or, in general, just try to pull you off your path to eventual healing.

The final third of people in your life will turn out to be truly supportive helpers. They will demonstrate a desire to understand you and the experience you are going through. They will be willing to be involved in your pain without feeling the need to take it away from you. They will believe in your capacity to integrate this divorce into your life and eventually go on to live a life of meaning and purpose.

Obviously, you want to seek out your friends and family who fall into this last third. They will be your confidants and momentum-givers on your journey.

How others can help you: three essentials

While there are a multitude of ways that people who care about you might reach out to help you, here are three important and fundamental helping roles. Effective helpers will help you:

1. **Feel "companioned" during your journey.** Someone who companions you is someone who is willing and able to affirm your pain and suffering. They are able to sit with you and the feelings that surface as you walk through the wilderness.

2. **Encounter your feelings related to the divorce transition.** These are people who understand the need for you to tell your account of your marriage and divorce. They ask you about your story and provide a safe place for you to openly express your many thoughts and feelings.

3. **Embrace hope.** These are people around you who help you sustain hope, even when you are in the middle of the wilderness of your divorce. They can be present to you and affirm your goodness, while all the time helping you trust in yourself that you can and will heal.

Support groups

You will probably discover, if you haven't already, that you can benefit from connecting with people who have also gone through a divorce. This "been there" factor is often the greatest benefit of divorce support groups. Coming together and sharing the common bond of experience can be invaluable in helping you heal. Knowing you are not alone when you feel like you are going crazy provides support and comfort.

In these groups, each person can talk about his or her experience in a non-threatening, safe atmosphere. Members offer each other support based on real life experience. Group members are usually very patient with you, and since they are not friends or family, can often have some outside perspective that is helpful to you.

You might think of divorce support groups as places where fellow journeyers gather. Each of you has a story to tell. Your wilderness stories help affirm the normalcy of each other's experiences. You also help each other build divine momentum toward healing.

Divorce support groups are available in many communities. They vary tremendously in their formats (open versus closed), durations, and content. If you are a candidate for one of these groups, do your research and find one that best meets your needs. While groups can be helpful, they are not for everyone. If in doubt, find a trusted confidant or counselor who can help you explore if this kind of experience might be of help to you.

To find a support group in your area, call your local mental health agency. Also, clergy, physicians, and attorneys will sometimes know about groups in your area.

Seek Integration—
Not Resolution

"It isn't for the moment you are struck that
you need courage, but for the long uphill
battle to faith, sanity and security."

Anne Morrow Lindbergh

How do you find your way out of the wilderness of your divorce experience? You don't have to dwell there forever, do you?

The good news is that like the millions who have gone before you, you can and will find your way out. But just as with any significant experience in your life, your divorce will always be a part of who you are and it will influence who you will become in the future.

You may be coming to understand one of the fundamental truths of the encounter with divorce transition: You don't wake up one day and magically feel "over it." *Integration* is a term I find appropriate for what occurs as you work to embrace the new reality of moving forward in life without your former spouse. With integration comes an ability to fully acknowledge the end of your marriage, feeling and acting like a single person with a future of your own design, a renewed sense of energy and confidence, and a capacity to become re-involved in the activities of life.

You will find that as you embrace this process of integration, the upheaval that comes with the wilderness will give rise to a new sense of meaning and purpose. Hope for a continued life will emerge as you are able to make commitments to your future. You can create an attitude and discover a desire to live a full life filled with gratitude and peace.

Signs of integration

How do you know if you are moving toward integrating your divorce into your life? As you move toward integration, you will begin to notice the following:

- A willingness to acknowledge that the divorce is happening (reality of the divorce) and that your relationship as a couple is over (finality of the divorce).
- A return to stable eating and sleeping patterns.
- Feeling and acting like a single person with a future of your own. You will have thoughts of your former spouse, but you will not be preoccupied by these thoughts.
- The capacity to enjoy experiences in life that are normally enjoyable.
- The establishment of both old and new friendships.

- The capacity to live a full life without feelings of guilt or lack of self-respect.
- The desire and capacity to plan your life toward the future.
- The serenity to become comfortable with the way things are rather than attempting to make things as they were.
- The versatility to welcome more change into your life.
- The awareness that you have allowed yourself to fully mourn, and you are still breathing—you have survived.
- The awareness that you don't completely "resolve" or "get over" your divorce; instead, you integrate it into your life.
- The acquaintance of new parts of yourself that you have discovered in your divorce journey.
- The adjustment to new role changes that have resulted from the divorce.
- The acknowledgment that the pain of loss is an inherent part of life resulting from the ability to give and receive love.
- A renewed sense of energy and confidence.
- The capacity to surround yourself with things that are nurturing to you.

Integration emerges much in the same way grass grows. Usually we don't check our lawns daily to see if the grass is growing, but it does grow, and soon we come to realize it is time to mow the grass again. Likewise, we don't look at ourselves each day of our divorce transition and see how we are healing. Yet we do come to realize, over the course of months, that we have come a long way. We have taken some important steps toward integration.

Usually there is not one great moment of arrival, but instead subtle changes and small advancements. It helps to have gratitude for even very small steps forward. If you mustered the energy to meet your friend for lunch, be grateful. If you had a good night's sleep, rejoice.

Of course, you will take some steps backward from time to time, but that is to be expected. Keep believing in yourself. Set your intention to integrate this divorce into your life journey and have hope that you can and will go on to have renewed meaning and purpose in our life.

Appreciate Your Transformation

"Sometimes a breakdown can be the beginning of a kind of breakthrough, a way of living in advance through a trauma that prepares you for a future of radical transformation."

Cherrie Moraga

The journey through divorce is life changing. When you leave the wilderness of your experience, you are simply not the same person as you were when you entered it. You have been through so much. How could you be the same?

I'm certain you have discovered that you have been transformed by your divorce journey. Many divorced people have said to me, "I have grown from this experience. I am a different person." You are indeed different now. You have likely grown in your wisdom, in your understanding, in your compassion.

Let me assure you that this book is not about advocating divorce as a means to growth, even though growth is often the result. It is about helping you do your mourning of lost dreams and helping you move toward a new, satisfying and meaningful life.

Divorce often frees good people from marriages that have been filled with unhappiness and dissatisfaction. Many people blossom in this new period of rediscovery of self. Divorce brings the freedom to explore pathways of change that you may have previously considered, but didn't think were possible.

Yes, divorce is a transition that teaches us more than we may have imagined possible. And, most of us who make it through this wilderness experience see ourselves as true survivors. We know something about life now that we may not have before. We can get more out of it. And, perhaps even more important, we discover how to give more, too!

Potential growth

To understand how transformation from divorce might occur in your life, let's explore some potential aspects of growth:

- **Growth means more meaning and purpose**
  Divorce seems to make us crave meaning and purpose in our everyday actions. Living life with meaning is the very opposite of just going through the motions of living. Giving attention to your divorce experience has a way of transforming your assumptions, values and priorities.

In part, purpose means living inside the question, "How can I discover my purpose for being in this world and fulfill that purpose?" Beyond that, it means being able to be a vital part of the universe, in harmony with something larger than yourself.

- **Growth means more energy and life force**
  When you integrate your divorce into your life, you unleash your inner power and divine spark—that which gives depth and purpose to your living. When you experience integration, you have more energy and enthusiasm for living.

  Now you can engage fully in life. Instead of letting life just happen to you, now you understand more, and your enhanced awareness unleashes energy to create your own destiny. Now you are not just existing, you are living abundantly.

- **Growth means more feelings**
  When you integrate your divorce into your life, you can experience your feelings more openly, honestly, and deeply. You are able to feel a full range of emotions, from sadness, protest, and anxiety to love, joy and passion. You become more authentic and alive.

- **Growth means more love, intimacy and connection**
  Mourning well your lost marriage relationship makes possible loving well in the future. You become a person you respect and value. Experiencing self-love allows you to receive the love you now open your heart to. You make yourself available and emanate a desire to connect deeply and intimately to those around you.

- **Growth means more possibilities**
  The integration of your divorce into your life opens you to a multitude of options. You may well discover an inner calling that invites you to follow your dreams. What have you always wanted to do but never did? What have you always told yourself was impossible? All that seemed impossible is now possible.

- **Growth means more satisfaction and fulfillment**
  Doing your divorce grief work allows you to discover your talents and gifts. By developing yourself and embracing your gifts, you feel fulfilled and one with the world around you. As you project a spiritual optimism into the world, you experience true satisfaction in living your life.

- **Growth means more truth**

  Making peace with your divorce invites you to live the truth. Living the truth is itself a journey into self-reflection and discovery. Surrender yourself to the truth, for to live your life in truth is to live in freedom.

- **Growth means more faith and spirituality**

  As you integrate your divorce into your life, you feel gratitude for what you have in life. The heart of faith is believing you are not alone. And now you realize you are not alone. You can see that life is a sacred journey and come to trust in the goodness that surrounds you.

- **Growth means transcendence**

  In transcending divorce, you find your higher self. As you emerge from the wilderness of your grief, you go above and beyond the life you have lived before and achieve a deeper understanding of the meaning and purpose of your life. You find self-fulfillment and realize your true potential.

My prayer for you

May you continue to discover the freedom to live life with purpose and meaning every moment of each day. May you turn your face to the radiance of joy. May you live in the continued awareness that you are being cradled in love by a caring presence that never deserts you. May you keep your heart open wide and be receptive to what life brings you, both happy and sad. And, in doing so, may you create a pathway to living your life fully and on purpose until you die. Blessings to you as you continue your life journey toward wholeness. May your divine spark shine brightly as you share your gifts with the universe.

I hope we meet one day.

The Divorced Person's Bill of Rights

Though you should reach out to others on your journey through divorce, you should not feel obliged to accept unhelpful responses you may receive from some people. You are the one who is going through this naturally difficult experience, and as such, you have certain "rights" no one should try to take away from you.

The following list is intended to empower you to heal and decide how others can and cannot help. This is not to discourage you from reaching out to others for help, but rather to assist you in distinguishing useful responses from hurtful ones.

1. *You have the right to experience your own unique divorce journey.* While you will discover some commonalities with other people going through divorce, no one will have the exact experience you do. So, when you turn to others for help, don't allow them to tell you what you should or should not be feeling.

2. *You have the right to talk about your divorce experience.* Talking about this major life transition will help you integrate it into your life. Be selective, but do find

people who are able and willing to listen to you as you move from head understanding to heart understanding of what you are experiencing.

3. *You have the right to feel a multitude of emotions.* It is important to befriend whatever feelings you are experiencing. Confusion, disorganization, fear, guilt, regret, sadness and relief are just a few of the emotions you might feel are a part of your divorce transition. Find listeners who will accept your feelings without condition.

4. *You have the right to be tolerant of your physical and emotional limits.* The divorce experience naturally leaves you feeling fatigued. Respect what your body, mind and heart are telling you. Get daily rest. Eat balanced meals. And don't allow others to push you into things you don't feel ready to do.

5. *You have the right to experience "griefbursts."* Sometimes, out of nowhere, powerful feelings of sadness and loss may overcome you. This can be frightening, but it is normal and natural. Find someone who understands and will let you talk it out.

6. *You have the right to make use of ceremony.* A divorce ceremony does more than acknowledge the end of your marriage. It helps provide you with the support of caring people. Look for compassionate resources and people to help you plan and carry out a ceremony to mark your major life change.

7. *You have the right to embrace your spirituality.* If faith is a part of your life, express it in ways that seem appropriate to you. Allow yourself to be around people who understand and support your religious or spiritual beliefs.

8. *You have the right to search for meaning.* You may find yourself asking, "Why my marriage? Where did things go wrong? Will life be worth living again?" Some of your questions may have answers; some may not. Just remember—those who do not question do not find.

9. *You have the right to seek and accept support during and after your divorce.* You cannot—nor should you try to—go through this time of major change alone. Remember, you need not walk alone. Look for a compassionate companion to accompany you on this difficult journey.

10. *You have the right to be transformed by your divorce.*
    Transformation means an entire change in form.
    You are indeed different now. You have likely grown
    in your wisdom, in your understanding, and in your
    compassion. As you integrate your divorce into your
    life, you will feel gratitude for your life.

About the author

Author, educator and grief counselor Dr. Alan Wolfelt is known across North America for his compassionate messages about healing in grief. He is committed to helping people mourn well so they can go on to live well and love well.

Dr. Wolfelt is founder and Director of the Center for Loss and Life Transition, located in the beautiful mountain foothills of Fort Collins, Colorado. Past recipient of the Association of Death Education and Counseling's Death Educator Award, he is also a faculty member of the University of Colorado Medical School's Department of Family Medicine.

Transcending Divorce

Ten Essential Touchstones for Finding Hope and Healing Your Heart

An expanded version of *The Wilderness of Divorce*

After years of being encouraged to contribute a book on divorce loss, Dr. Wolfelt has responded with this compassionate new guide. When it comes to grief and loss, divorce is one of the most heartbreaking for many people.

With empathy and wisdom, Dr. Wolfelt walks the reader through ten essential Touchstones for hope and healing. Readers are encouraged to give attention to the need to mourn their lost relationship before "moving on" to a new relationship.

If you're hurting after a divorce, this book is for you. Warm, direct and easy to understand, this is a book you will not want to put down.

ISBN 978-1-879651-50-0 • 195 pages • softcover • $14.95

The Transcending Divorce Journal

Exploring the Ten Essential Touchstones

For many people, journaling is an excellent way to process the many painful thoughts and feelings after a divorce. While private and independent, journaling is still the outward expression of grief. And it is through the outward expression of grief that healing begins.

This companion journal to *Transcending Divorce* helps you explore the ten essential touchstones for finding hope and healing your grieving heart after divorce. Throughout, you will be reminded of the content you have read in the companion book and asked corresponding questions about your unique grief journey. This compassionate journal provides you with ample space to unburden your heart and soul.

ISBN 978-1-879651-54-8 • 134 pages • softcover • $14.95

The Transcending Divorce Support Group Guide

Guidance and Meeting Plans for Facilitators

When we are experiencing feelings of grief and loss during and after a divorce, we need the support and compassion of our fellow human beings. Divorce support groups provide an opportunity for this healing kind of support.

This book is for those who want to facilitate an effective divorce group. It includes 12 meeting plans that interface with Dr. Wolfelt's *Transcending Divorce* book and its companion journal. Each week, group members read a portion of *Transcending Divorce* and write down their thoughts and feelings in the guided journal. Using the *Support Group Guide* in conjunction with the other two texts, support group leaders can simply and effectively combine divorce grief education with compassionate support—all in a practical, 12-meeting structure.

ISBN 978-1-879651-56-2 • 60 pages • softcover • $12.95

Living in the Shadow of the Ghosts of Grief
Step into the Light

Reconcile old losses and open the door to infinite joy and love

Are you depressed? Anxious? Angry? Do you have trouble with trust and intimacy? Do you feel a lack of meaning and purpose in your life? You may well be *Living in the Shadow of the Ghosts of Grief*.

When you suffer a loss of any kind—whether through abuse, divorce, job loss, the death of someone loved or other transitions, you naturally grieve inside. To heal your grief, you must express it. That is, you must mourn your grief. If you don't, you will carry your grief into your future, and it will undermine your happiness for the rest of your life.

This compassionate guide will help you learn to identify and mourn your carried grief so you can go on to live the joyful, whole life you deserve.

ISBN 978-1-879651-51-7 • 160 pages • softcover • $13.95